Cambridge Contemporary Poets 1

Edited by

Wes Magee

CAMBRIDGE
UNIVERSITY PRESS

Published by the Press Syndicate of the University of Cambridge
The Pitt Building, Trumpington Street, Cambridge CB2 1RP
40 West 20th Street, New York, NY 10011-4211 USA
10 Stamford Road, Oakleigh, Victoria, 3166, Australia

A catalogue record for this book is available from the
British Library.

Printed in Great Britain at the University Press, Cambridge

ISBN 0 521 39749 9 paperback

Cover and text photography by Nicholas Judd

V N

Contents

Wes Magee

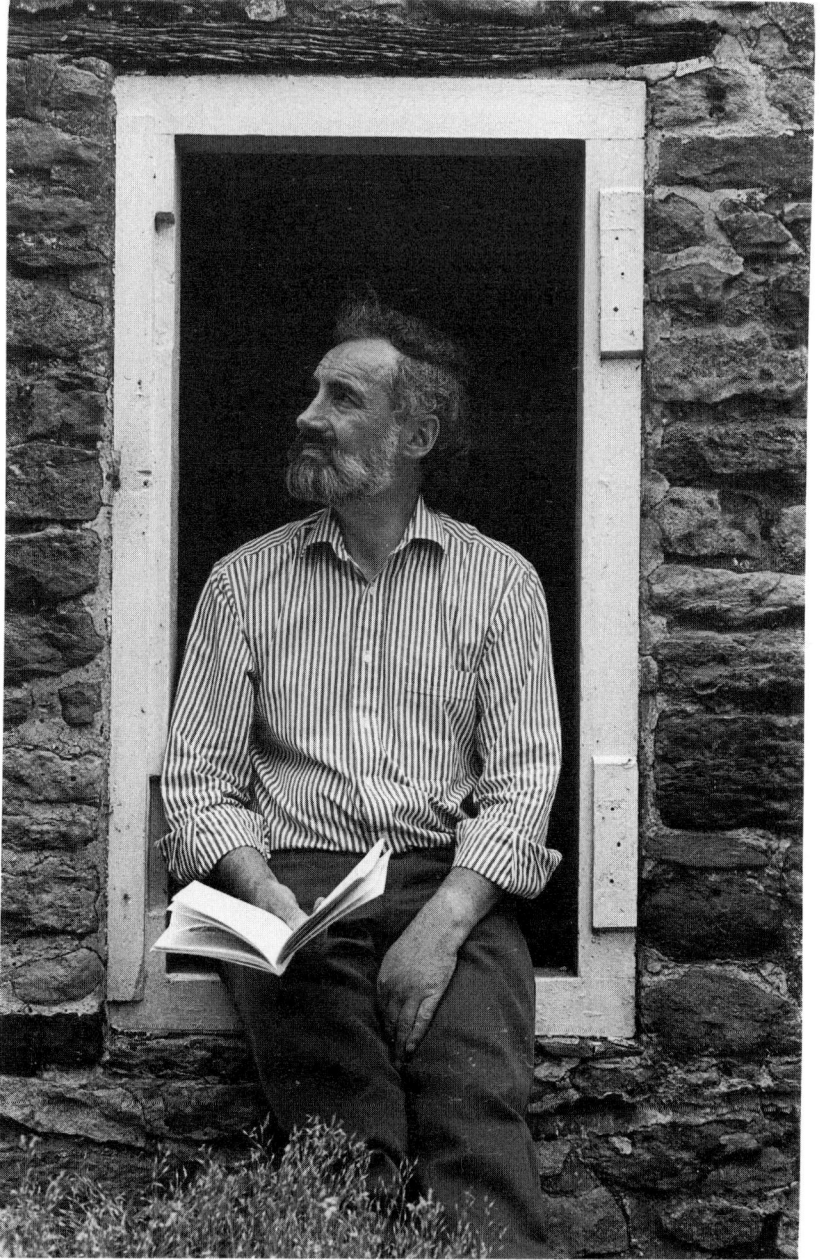

Editor's introduction

The great poets of the past, writers like William Shakespeare, John Keats or Alfred, Lord Tennyson, are household names and their poems are part of a rich literary tradition. Yet poetry doesn't belong solely to the past. Writers of the present day seek to add to that long tradition by producing poems appropriate to our own life and times.

The eight contemporary poets included here come from differing backgrounds and each contributor has written an introduction to show how she or he developed an interest in poetry. Mostly, when we read a book, we are only vaguely aware of *who* the author is. In this book there is opportunity to know more about the authors and to learn how they go about the task of communicating with the reader.

The poems in *Cambridge Contemporary Poets 1*, like the writers, differ greatly. Some poems are humorous, some are serious. You will read poems that tell a story or relate an experience, while others observe people or recall an incident from childhood. Whether the poems are long or short, each piece of writing offers a new beginning, a fresh outlook for the reader. So, open the book and – as they say in the USA – 'enjoy!'

Wes Magee

Gareth Owen

Introduction

I was born and brought up in Ainsdale, Lancashire. Both parents were Welsh and a mixture of Welsh and English was spoken at home. My mother died when I was one and a half. My father was a bank clerk but was very interested in books and literature. There were lots of books in the house and I read a great deal, mainly the classics of the time: *Treasure Island*, *Black Beauty*, *Swallows and Amazons*, *Lorna Doone* and the *Just William* books. There were also encyclopædias and three large books called *The World's Greatest Paintings*. There were comics: *Adventure*, *Hotspur*, *Film Fun*, *Beano*.

My father was a devout Methodist and deacon of the local Welsh Chapel. We went to Chapel three times a week. On Sunday you had to wear your best clothes and not play cards or noisy games or listen to the radio unless it was a religious programme. Welsh religious services are much more emotional and dramatic than those in England. The sermons are passionate and theatrical while the hymns are poetic, dark and uplifting. That oratory and spiritual force is in my blood. I'm not religious now but I still have a longing for some kind of eternity, a land that is always just out of sight. This probably accounts for the melancholy side of me. From the Lancashire side I get my sense of comic realism. Whenever I write something I consider to be good I know it's because these contradictory parts of my nature have come together.

I was a bit of a failure at school. The only subjects I was good at were English and football. My ambition was to play for Everton. I also thought it wouldn't be half bad being a film producer in Hollywood. At maths and science I was hopeless. In one exam I got three per cent for algebra. My teacher remarked with a kind of bewildered admiration that this was probably a world record. The days when I took my school reports home were nightmares.

By a miracle I managed to scrape four O-levels together and at sixteen I joined the Merchant Navy. It soon became obvious to me that I would never make Admiral of the Fleet. The calculations involved in navigation were beyond me. Once I plotted that our ship was steaming down Shaftesbury Avenue. After three years, to the Navy's relief, I quit. Falling off a mast in Buenos Aires and sustaining a triple fracture of the skull didn't help either.

9

For three years I did various dead-end jobs before being accepted at Bretton Hall teacher training college in Yorkshire. I loved it. I did drama and my compulsion to always play the fool paid dividends as an actor. I also found my contrariness led to my expressing original opinions in essays. Suddenly all those parts of my character which had been drawbacks seemed to be useful. For the first time I was successful at something.

The writing began in this way. I could find few poems that reflected the ordinary interests of the children I was teaching, so I started writing my own. Soon I had about thirty poems knocking about. I never thought to send them to a publisher. Being published was something that happened to other people. By chance I met Barry Maybury at a teachers' course in Oxford. He was putting together an anthology and included five of my poems. This was in 1970. It encouraged me to offer my collection to other publishers but after two rejections I gave up and began writing plays for a local pub theatre company. Over the next eight years I wrote sixteen plays, three of which were produced in America. A director suggested I send my poems to Penguin Books and, wonder of wonders, they agreed to publish. *Salford Road* appeared in 1979, seventeen years after the poems had been written! Soon I had enough poems for a second book. I bought a second-hand typewriter and prepared a neat manuscript and sent it round. Collins Publishers were the first to reply. Thus, in 1985, *Song of the City* was published. It won the Signal Poetry Award and has gone to five reprints.

My first novel, *The Final Test* appeared in 1985. I breathed a sigh of relief when it was done. Then my editor asked me what my next book was going to be about. I hadn't even thought of a *next* book! *The Man With Eyes Like Windows* appeared in 1987 and *Saving grace* in 1989. My fourth novel, *Omelette*, appeared in 1990. It's all astonished me. When people refer to me as 'the writer' I look over my shoulder and wonder who they're talking about. The more I write, the harder it seems to get. It's like digging. I always have a strange feeling that my novel already exists. I have to find it; go digging for it.

Do I enjoy it? It's good when it's over. When I look at 130 pages of typed manuscript I allow myself a couple of seconds of pride. Then I begin to think: 'What's the next book going to be about? Will there even be one?'

I hope so. Watch this space.

FACT FILE

Birthplace	Ainsdale, Lancashire
Brothers/sisters	One sister
School	Merchant Taylors', Crosby
Further education	Bretton Hall College, Yorkshire and Goldsmiths' College, London
Favourite sport	Soccer (support Everton)
Musical interest	Soul. Write country songs. Play electric keyboard (badly)
Favourite food	Italian
Favourite drink	Shandy ... on a hot day
Best TV programme	'Bilko', also 'Match of the Day'
Best radio programme	'Hancock's Half Hour'
Travels abroad	USA, South America, France, Spain, Italy
Favourite book (as a child)	*Black Beauty* by Anna Sewell
Favourite poets	William Shakespeare, John Donne, Byron, Browning, T. S. Eliot, Philip Larkin and many more
Comment on 'green' issues	It is the *only* issue
Hobbies	Records, song writing, gardening, watching football, acting, directing
Ambition	To write one good book, and then another, and then another, and then ...
Pets	Cat called 'Rubble'
Preferred transport	Car

Salford Road

Salford Road, Salford Road,
Is the place where I was born,
With a green front gate, a red brick wall
And hydrangeas round a lawn.

Salford Road, Salford Road,
Is the road where we would play
Where the sky lay over the roof tops
Like a friend who'd come to stay.

The Gardeners lived at fifty-five,
The Lunds with the willow tree,
Mr Pool with the flag and the garden pond
And the Harndens at fifty-three.

There was riding bikes and laughing
Till we couldn't laugh any more,
And bilberries picked on the hillside
And picnics on the shore.

I lay in bed when I was four
As the sunlight turned to grey
And heard the train through my pillow
And the seagulls far away.

And I rose to look out of my window
For I knew that someone was there
And a man stood as sad as nevermore
And didn't see me there.

And when I stand in Salford Road
And think of the boy who was me
I feel that from one of the windows
Someone is looking at me.

My friends walked out one Summer day,
Walked singing down the lane,
My friends walked into a wood called Time
And never came out again.

We live in a land called Gone-Today
That's made of bricks and straw
But Salford Road runs through my head
To a land called Evermore.

My sister Betty

My sister Betty said,
'I'm going to be a famous actress,'
Last year she was going to be a missionary.
'Famous actresses always look unhappy but beautiful,'
She said, pulling her mouth sideways
And making her eyes turn upwards
So they were mostly white.
'Do I look unhappy but beautiful?'
'I want to go to bed and read,' I said.
'Famous actresses suffer and have hysterics,' she said.
'I've been practising my hysterics.'
She began going very red and screaming
So that it hurt my ears.
She hit herself on the head with her fists
And rolled off my bed on to the lino.
I stood by the wardrobe where it was safer.
She got up saying, 'Thank you, thank you,'
And bowed to the four corners of my bedroom.
'Would you like an encore of hysterics?' she asked.
'No,' I said from inside the wardrobe.
There was fluff all over her vest.
'If you don't clap enthusiastically,' she said,
'I'll put your light out when you're reading.'
While I clapped a bit
She bowed and shouted, 'More, more!'
Auntie Gwladys shouted upstairs,
'Go to bed and stop teasing Betty.'
'The best thing about being a famous actress,' Betty said,
'Is that you get to die a lot.'
She fell to the floor with a crash
And lay there for an hour and a half
With her eyes staring at the ceiling.
She only went away when I said,
'You really look like a famous actress
Who's unhappy but beautiful.'

When I got into bed and started reading,
She came and switched off my light.
It's not much fun
Having a famous actress for a sister.

Song of the city

My brain is stiff with concrete
My limbs are rods of steel
My belly's stuffed with money
My soul was bought in a deal.

They poured metal through my arteries
They choked my lungs with lead
They churned my blood to plastic
They put murder into my head.

I'd a face like a map of the weather
Flesh that grew to the bone
But they tore my story out of my eyes
And turned my heart to stone.

Let me wind from my source like a river
Let me grow like wheat from the grain
Let me hold out my arms like a natural tree
Let my children love me again.

Out in the city

When you're out in the city
Shuffling down the street,
A bouncy city rhythm
Starts to boogie in your feet.

It jumps off the pavement,
There's a snare drum in your brain,
It pumps through your heart
Like a diesel train.

There's Harry on the corner,
Sings, 'How she goin' boy?'
To loose and easy Winston
With his brother Leroy.

Shout, 'Hello!' to Billy Brisket
With his tripes and cows heels,
Blood-stained rabbits
And trays of live eels.

Maltese Tony
Smoking in the shade
Keeping one good eye
On the amusement arcade.

And everybody's talking:

Move along
Step this way
Here's a bargain
What you say?
Mind your backs
Here's the stop
More fares?
Room on top.

WEN • GARETH OWEN • GARETH OWEN • GARETH OWEN • GARETH OWEN • GARET

Neon lights and take-aways
Gangs of boys and girls
Football crowds and market stalls
Taxi cabs and noise.

From the city cafes
On the smoky breeze
Smells of Indian cooking
Greek and Cantonese.

Well, some people like suburban life
Some people like the sea
Others like the countryside
But it's the city
Yes it's the city
It's the city life
For me.

A dog's life

Waking up last Friday and dressing for school
I found I'd turned into a dog.
I looked at myself in the glass.
Same Ben with glasses and broken tooth stared back
But I just knew I was an alsatian.
'You're an alsatian,' I said to my reflection.
'Woof woof,' my reflection barked back.
No doubt about it, I was an alsatian.
I rushed into the bathroom
Where my sister was cleaning her teeth.
'I'm an alsatian,' I barked happily,
'My name's Attila.'
'Stop being stupid,' she said. 'I'm late for school.'
I sank my teeth into this piece of leg
That came out of a nightie.
'Good dog Attila,' she agreed.
I chased downstairs on all fours
Barking joyfully;
Being an alsatian called Attila agreed with me.
My new life came as a surprise to my mother
Since I have two sisters, a brother and a father
And not one of them is an alsatian.
'Good morning,' I barked to my mother and father
Giving a big grin and letting my tongue loll out.
'I'm an alsatian,' I said,
Standing on my back legs on the chair
And resting my paws in the All Bran.
'Stop dribbling and eat your breakfast properly,'
Said my mother.
'Woof woof,' I explained from my place under the sofa
Trying to eat a sausage without using my front paws.
'Your son's an alsatian,' said my mother.
'Dr McEever said we might see a sudden improvement,'
Said my father from behind his newspaper.
After the first shock, they soon got used to the idea
Of having a dog with spectacles called Attila
About the house;
Parents can be very adaptable

If you give them a chance.
It's a good life now,
A dog's life.
There's less homework, I don't have to shut doors
And I have my own place on a mat by the fire.
I spend my days sniffing and looking purposeful.
Some days I bury motor bikes
Or bits of sideboard in the cabbage patch.
Baby Sophie likes me a lot;
She gurgles and chuckles as I lick her face
Or try to herd the tortoise into her playpen.
Suddenly I feel wanted.
My family speak to me a lot now
And are learning what my barks mean.
'Good boy Attila,' they say and tickle my ears.
My father spends hours taking me for walks
Or throwing sticks for me to bring back in my jaws.
And then to hear my mother calling
On some sunlit afternoon,
'Attila, Attila, time for cubs.'
And I romp up from the garden my tail wagging,
Weaving between the apple trees
And the white sheets on the line.
Well, there's nothing like it.
You really should try it sometime.

In Henley library

Miss Goodman stands behind the polished counter
Stamping books.
Her hair is frizzed and orange
And she wears a face
That's somewhere in between
A simper and a smile.
'These books are late,' she says
As if somehow the guilt lay with the books
Although of course it's me
Who has to pay the fine.
I hand across the thirty pence
That otherwise I would have spent
On polo mints and aniseeds.
The library smells of calor gas
And castle walls.
As always, the strange old lady
In the plastic pixie hat is there;
She shuffles, head up, frowning,
Searching the spines
In the section marked 'Romance'.
Above it is a poster
Warning you of AIDS;
'Don't take the risk,' it says.
Does that apply to everything?
I make for 'Stories'.
Outside the cars roar
Through the rain on Henley High Street.
In here I'm in a hundred different worlds;
Retrieving magic rings in Middle Earth,
Or in the fifth form at Saint Clare's
Bolting my secret dormitory feast
With Isobel and Pat
Before Ma'moiselle comes round
To call lights out.
And then again
My trusty Hurricane
(One wing a scarf of flame)
Limps bravely home through streams of flak

20

That flare up from the Dardanelles.
But someone, somewhere taps the message out;
'We will be back.'
Oh mother we'll be back,
With Love and Blood and Wild Adventure
'Neath our arms
Striding through the rain-dashed faces and the feet
Past shop fronts bright ablaze with lights
And faceless dummies staring at the street.
We will be back
Oh mother do not fret
We do this every week now
And it hasn't killed us yet.

Judith Nicholls

Introduction

'What made you want to be a poet?' I am often asked after talking to a hall-full of pupils and teachers in schools. The strange thing is that I first wrote as a teenager because I was quite terrified of speaking to any more than one (friendly) person at a time! Paper was safer. I could spend as long as I wanted working out what to say and how to say it; no one need see or hear those words unless I *chose* to share them.

The poems I wrote at that time were not good – though of course secretly I thought they were brilliant! They were mainly variations on Great Thoughts on Life and Death; it wasn't until many years later that I discovered that simpler poems could be much more effective, even to express very complex ideas.

Another thing I learned was that a poem is *made*. This sounds very obvious. Yet whilst no one would dream of throwing a lump of clay on to the table and announcing they had 'made' a dish or a castle, it's surprising how many people think they can throw a pile of words on to a page and announce they have made a poem!

When I work in schools I always show the drafts of one of my recent poems. Published ones always look so neat and simple; even adults often don't realise the mess that preceded the final version. Here, for example, is the last verse of a simple poem I wrote about 'Winter':

> *Winter raced
> down the frozen stream,
> catching at his breath;
> on his lips were icicles,
> at his back was death.

This little verse took *twenty or thirty* different attempts until I had the one I wanted.

My first real batch of 'crafted' poems – ten of them – were sent out towards the end of 1983 and seven of them were accepted for an Oxford University Press anthology. It was several days before I came down off the ceiling – and several more before I realised there was little point in sitting back for a couple of years until the book was actually in print. Gradually, I began to learn the *discipline* of the writer's trade; gradually, what had become a hobby was now, to my amazement, to become a full-time job.

I work from home, which is a cottage in a Wiltshire churchyard. My study would be a tidy parent's despair, with every horizontal and vertical surface covered with books, pencils, files, notes, paintings, general paperwork... I usually know roughly where to find what I need, but few would believe it from the general appearance.

Ambitions? *One* day it would be satisfying to have an *organised* filing system! Apart from that, I'd love to be able to illustrate a book of my own, though this is very much a 'pipe-dream' as I'm easily the worst in my art class.

At the moment, my time is divided between writing and giving readings and running workshops in schools and with teachers. At the time of writing I have worked with almost two hundred different schools, from Cornwall to Suffolk, Jersey to Lincolnshire, London to California. I enjoy helping people to enjoy poetry and feel especially pleased when I hear pupils saying to each other at the end of the afternoon things like, 'Cor! That was much better than PE', 'I didn't think I liked poetry before!', or when parents say to me, '*I'm* going to go home and try writing a poem now!'

And so they should; poetry is *fun*.

* 'Winter' from *Midnight forest* by Judith Nicholls (Faber & Faber)

·F A C T·
·F I L E·

Birthplace	Westwoodside, Lincolnshire
Brothers/sisters	One sister
School	Junior school in Skegness, and then Skegness Grammar School
Further Education	Teacher training college (Salisbury); Hons. degree in education (Bristol University)
Favourite sport	Swimming, walking
Musical interest	Listening to a wide variety of music
Favourite food	Home-made wholemeal bread and soups, bananas, fresh dates, carrot cake
Favourite drink	Freshly-squeezed orange juice
Best TV programme	'Cheers'
Best radio programme	'PM'
Travels abroad	France (often), Spain, Portugal (lived there for a year), USA, Italy, Morocco, Germany
Favourite book (as a child)	*The River* by Rumer Godden
Favourite poets	e. e. cummings, Roger McGough, Charles Causley, Emily Dickinson, Grace Nichols, Kit Wright
Comment on 'green' issues	Vitally important
Hobbies	Going to art classes (drawing, and painting), walking, sailing
Ambitions	To get organised ... one day. And to do a book with my own illustrations
Pets	Used to own a cat called 'Sooty'
Preferred transport	Feet ... then train

Countdown

'Hurry,' cried Progress,
and on to Earth
rushed

chain saw, axe and JCB,
crop sprays, oil slicks, pesticide;
battery farms and DDT,
smog and tear gas, monoxide.
Additives and sonic boom,
pills and parking lots,
concrete jungles, filled with gloom,
high-rise concrete flats.
Nuclear waste for just a taste
of what is still to come;
settle down, our shelter's warm –
do make yourself at home!
We've cigarettes to blacken lungs –
never mind the bill;
who needs seeds and forestry
with acid rain to kill?

'Come in, come in!' cried Progress,
'Let's light these cloudy skies –'
and crept towards the button,
rubbing smoke-filled eyes.

'Welcome, daughters,
to your land –
this ark is yours and mine.
Do watch your step,
the trap is set –
we only wait for Time.

Come in, my sons,
do feel at home;
come in and share the mirth!
I've played my part –
you alone
can rescue planet Earth.'

Moonscape

No air, no mist, no man, no beast.
No water flows from her Sea of Showers,
no trees, no flowers fringe her Lake of Dreams.
No grass grows or clouds shroud her high hills
or deep deserts. No whale blows in her dry Ocean of Storms.

A poem for the rainforest

Song of the Xingu Indian

They have stolen my land;
the birds have flown,
my people gone.
My rainbow rises over sand;
my river falls on stone.

Amazonian Timbers, Inc.

This can go next –
here, let me draw the line.
That's roughly right,
give or take
a few square miles or so.
I'll list the ones we need.
No, burn the rest.
Only take the best,
we're not in this
for charity.
Replant? No –
you're new to this, I see!
There's plenty more
where that comes from,
no problem! Finish here –
and then move on.

Dusk

Butterfly, blinded
by smoke, drifts like torn paper
to the flames below.

Shadows

Spider,
last of her kind,
scuttles underground, safe;
prepares her nest for young ones. But
none come.

The coming of night

Sun sinks
behind the high canopy;
the iron men are silenced.

The moon rises,
the firefly wakes.
Death pauses for a night.

Song of the forest

*Our land has gone,
our people flown.
Sun scorches our earth,
our river weeps.*

Give me your name!

Give me your name, and I will...

whisper it into the forests,
spell it out in the sands,
I'll shout it over the thunder,
breathe it away on the wind.
I'll spill it over the mountains,
let it echo through the rain;
I'll sing it into a seashell,
if you give me your name.

Hermitage Woods

Who was the hermit of Hermitage Woods,
and why did he walk alone?
Was his bed of moss and his roof a star,
was his pillow stone?

Was the hoot of the owl his lullaby,
the wind in the oak his song?
Was the moon his only candle,
when day was done?

Who was the hermit of Hermitage Woods,
and why was he there?
When he smiled, who shared his laughter;
when he cried, who could hear?

Was the scent of pine in his winter breath?
Did his eyes burn with the sun?
What taste of mists swirled in his throat
and round his tongue?

Who *was* the hermit of Hermitage Woods,
who walked at dusk and dawn?
Where are the oaks which sheltered him?
Where has he gone?

The dare

Go on, I dare you,
come on down!

Was it *me* they called?
Pretend you haven't heard,
a voice commanded in my mind.
Walk past, walk fast
and don't look down,
don't look behind.

Come on, it's easy!

The banks were steep,
the water low
and flanked with oozing brown.
Easy? Walk fast
but don't look down.
Walk straight, walk on,
even risk their jeers
and run . . .

Never go near those dykes,
my mother said.
No need to tell me.
I'd seen stones sucked in
and covered without trace,
gulls slide to bobbing safety,
grasses drown as water rose.
No need to tell me
to avoid the place.

She ca-a-a-n't, she ca-a-a-n't!
Cowardy, cowardy custard!

There's no such word as 'can't',
my father said.
I slowed my pace.
The voices stopped,
waited as I wavered, grasping breath.
My mother's wrath? My father's scorn?
A watery death?

I hesitated then turned back,
forced myself to see the mud below.
After all, it was a dare...
There was no choice;
I had to go.

Charles Causley

Introduction

I was born at Launceston, a small market-town in north
Cornwall, and I still make my home there. The Kensey (a
tributary of the Tamar) runs by Riverside, the group of cottages
in one of which I was born. A hundred yards away is a medieval
pack-bridge (we fished from there), St Thomas Church and
churchyard, and also the ruins of an Augustinian priory.
Underlane – half a mile distant – has the remains of the 1897
Diamond Jubilee Swimming Bath, now closed, set in the long
river valley of splendid fields and meadows. The whole town is
presided over by a stern-looking Norman castle. All these places
are where I acted out my childhood and most of them, at one
time or another, have entered my poems.

My father had been a soldier in France in the 1914–18 War,
returned an invalid, and died when I was seven. Despite being an
only child, I was never conscious of being lonely. Besides my
school friends there seemed dozens of cousins, aunts and uncles.
I discovered the world of books early on, and read everything I
could get hold of.

I always wanted to be a writer, and wrote a lot (mostly poems
and plays) when I was in my teens. I also had piano lessons and
from the ages of 14 to 21 played in a local four-piece dance-
band. During the daytime I worked in a succession of offices. I
found the work stupefyingly boring and wondered if I'd ever
escape.

In 1940, when I joined the Royal Navy, I decided that if I
survived the war I would train as a teacher, and this is what
happened. All through my six wartime years I read (particularly)
a lot of poetry and tried to improve my own, but I made no
serious attempt at publishing anything until I was a civilian
again. My principal aim was always to become a writer, if
possible a poet, but it seemed unlikely that one could make a
living out of poetry. I had the idea that as a teacher I would be
able to spend long periods in writing during the holidays, but I
rarely did. In practice, I found it more useful to work steadily at
a little poetry every day, if I could.

Before 1940, nobody told me that you simply wrote about
what you knew, and my home-town in those days didn't seem to
offer much in the way of theme and subject. (I don't think so

today.) I thought poetry lived somewhere else; not under my nose. It was during the war and the course of a totally new existence, with its experiences of separation and loss – particularly the loss of comrades – that I first tried to write about what was happening around me.

I didn't manage to become a full-time writer until I was in my fifties and had published a fair number of books.

Today, I spend a lot of my spare time travelling in other countries, but I never fail to enjoy returning to Cornwall. I don't go in search of subjects or ideas. I think that, on the contrary, these should somehow seek out the writer. One can't write poems all the time, and there's a lot to be said, in a 'dry' writing season, for trying to keep one's nerve and letting the field lie fallow for a while. I also try to remember some words of the German poet Goethe: 'We must be right by nature, so that good thoughts might come before us like free children of God and say, "Here we are".'

I've never planned to write a prose autobiography. With luck, it's all in the poems.

FACT FILE

Birthplace	Launceston, Cornwall
Favourite sport	Swimming
Favourite books (as a child)	Abridged versions of *David Copperfield* and *Treasure Island*. The *William* books. Conan Doyle's *The White Company*
Favourite poets	William Shakespeare, Thomas Hardy, W. H. Auden, Philip Larkin, Ted Hughes
Hobbies	Plays and films
Pets	Cats

Forbidden games

A lifetime, and I see them still:
My aunt, my mother, silently
Held by the stove's unflinching eye
Inside the tall house scaled with slate.
The paper boy runs up the hill,
Cries 'Echo!' to the black-blown sky.
The tin clock on the kitchen shelf
Taps seven. And I am seven. And lie
Flat on the floor playing a game
Of Snakes & Ladders by myself.

Upstairs, my father in his bed,
Shadowed still by the German War,
A thin light burning at his head,
To me is no more than a name
That's also mine. I wonder what
The two women are waiting for.
My aunt puts down her library book.
My mother winds a bit of wool.
Each gives to each a blinded look.
'Your father's with the angels now.'
Which of them speaks I cannot tell.
And then I say to them, 'I know.'
And give the dice another throw.

My enemy

My enemy was the pork butcher's son.
I see him, head and shoulders over me,
Sphinx-faced, his cheeks the colour of lard, the eyes
Revolver-blue through Bunter spectacles.
When we lined up for five to nine at school
He'd get behind me, crumple up a fist,
Stone thumb between the first and second fingers;
Punch out a tune across my harp of ribs.

Ten years ahead of Chamberlain, I tried
Appeasement, with the same results: gave him
My lunch of bread and cheese, the Friday bun,
The Lucky Bags we bought at Maggie Snell's.
One Armistice I wept through the Two Minutes
Because my dad was killed in France (not true).
'Poor little sod, his father's dead,' my enemy
Observed, discreetly thumping me again.

I took the scholarship exam not for
The promise of Latin, Greek, but to escape
My enemy. The pork butcher's sharp son
Passed too, and I remember how my heart
Fell like a bucket down a summer well
The day Boss Ward read out our names. And how,
Quite unaccountably, the torment stopped
Once we were at the Grammar. We've not met

Since 1939, although I heard
How as a gunner in the long retreat
Hauling the piece from Burma, he was met
At the first village by naked kids with stones,
Placards reading 'Quit India'. After that,
Nothing; except our pair of sentences
To thirty years in chalk Siberias:
Which one of us is which hard to define
For children in the butcher's class, and mine.

Logs of wood

When in the summer sky the sun
Hung like a golden ball,
John Willy from the Workhouse came
And loudly he would bawl:

Wood! Wood! Logs of wood
To keep out the cold!
Shan't be round tomorrow!
They all must be sold!

But O the sky was shining blue
And green was the spray.
It seemed as if the easy days
Would never pass away.

And when John Willy came to town
The laughter it would start,
And we would smile as he went by
Pushing his wooden cart.

John Willy, I can see you still,
Coming down Tower Street,
Your pointed nose, your cast-off clothes,
Your Charlie Chaplin feet.

And like the prophet you would stand
Calling loud and long,
But there were few who listened to
The story of your song.

Wood! Wood! Logs of wood
To keep out the cold!
Shan't be round tomorrow!
They all must be sold!

But now the snow is on the hill,
The ice is on the plain,
And dark as dark a shadow falls
Across my window-pane.

Tomorrow, ah, tomorrow –
That name I did not fear
Until Tomorrow came and said,
Good morrow. I am here.

At St Hilary

Between two Cornish seas, the spire
Blazes the land, the waving air.

The dark stem of a Celtic cross
Sprouts, half-grown, from the shallow grass.

A tomb, exploded, shows the bones
Of a young sycamore. Slant stones

Cram the graveyard like ships stormbound.
A wasted urn drips shard and sand.

Like auguries, two seabirds lie
Motionless in the squalling sky.

Through rain and wind and risen snow
I come, as fifty years ago,

Drawn by I know not what, to sound
A fabled shore, unlost, unfound,

Where in the shadow of the sun
Past, present, future, wait as one.

Only the breathing ash speaks true.
Nothing is new. Nothing is new

As the sea slinks to where I stand
Between the water and the land.

Tom Bone

My name is Tom Bone,
I live all alone
In a deep house on Winter Street.
  Through my mud wall
  The wolf-spiders crawl
  And the mole has his beat.

On my roof of green grass
All the day footsteps pass
In the heat and the cold,
  As snug in a bed
  With my name at its head
  One great secret I hold.

Tom Bone, when the owls rise
In the drifting night skies
Do you walk round about?
  All the solemn hours through
  I lie down just like you
  And sleep the night out.

Tom Bone, as you lie there
On your pillow of hair,
What grave thoughts do you keep?
  Tom says, Nonsense and stuff!
  You'll know soon enough.
  Sleep, darling, sleep.

Gerda Mayer

Introduction

I was born in Karlsbad, Czechoslovakia. Our local football team
kept getting beaten every Sunday, which so depressed my father
that he took me on Sunday rambles instead. I owe a great deal
of happiness to that football team. I saw mountains, meadows,
forests, lakes. My father was fun and he was extremely fond of
me; he keeps cropping up in my poems.

It was my mother, though, who gave me poetry. She was very
good at reading it aloud, and she wrote some herself. Walking in
the park, one day, we stopped in front of a statue. 'That's
Goethe,' my mother said in tones of reverence. We stood quietly
before the statue of the famous German poet, as if it were some
wayside shrine.

My own first recorded poem (which my parents entered into a
diary) was composed at the age of four. In fact, I have written
verse ever since I can remember. My early poems were seldom
much good and I improved only when I learnt to revise.

I was enormously stage-struck when I was a child and my
parents encouraged me to learn poems by heart and to recite
them in public. I saw it as a substitute for acting. Without
realising it, I was also absorbing the sounds and rhythms of
language. The acting stopped after I came to England in 1939, at
the age of eleven.

Hitler had invaded the German part of Czechoslovakia in 1938
and we, being Jews, had had to flee to Prague, the capital. There
my parents tried desperately to emigrate, but to no avail.
However, some wonderfully generous British people began to
organise children's transports, and so helped some of us to
escape to this country. I was one of the lucky ones and flew to
England in the company of other children in March 1939. I
wasn't to know that I would never see my parents again and
regarded my coming here as a great adventure.

Ten days after my arrival, I wrote in my diary . . .

24th March 1939

Dear Diary,

I am sure you will have been surprised by your
new surroundings. For I have taken you along
with me to England. It was lovely on the plane
but I was twice sick. Now I really am in England.
I was sick on the plane and even sicker in the
car. I thought I was going to murderers who
wanted to abduct me. Then when we got out to
drink milk I became more cheerful...

I led quite a nomadic life in England, moving from prep. school
to a state school and then on to a truly horrendous boarding
school. Luckily this closed when I was fifteen, and I spent my last
two years at school at an enchanting boarding school in Surrey,
where poetry flourished.

FACT FILE

Birthplace	Karlsbad, Czechoslovakia
Brothers/sisters	One sister
School	8, or 9 different schools
Further education	Bedford College, University of London
Favourite sport	Swimming, walking
Travels abroad	European countries, Israel
Favourite books (as a child)	*Little Lord Fauntleroy*, *Dr Doolittle*
Comment on 'green' issues	I wrote conservation poems long before they became fashionable
Hobbies	Visiting art galleries
Ambition	To have my obituary in *The Times*
Pets	Ginger cat called 'Ginger'

Fragment

My father lifted
a mouthorgan up
to the wind on a hill

and the wind of Bohemia
sighed a few
frail and blue notes

man and child
in a harebell light
frail ghosts ... faint tune

Hide and seek

Once I used to hide
in the open recess
under the first
floor balcony,
(*and always*,
my father remarked,
in the same place).

Where can she be?
Where can she be?
Here comes my aunt
searching and thin
and walks past me the first time;
this being the ritual.

Forty years later
and the recess
has shrunk to
under my chin;
and is full of
old lumber now and
a better place to hide in.
I look into the shadows
and ask and ask
where are they?

Star of sorrow
Star of a dark night
We wear you on our arms

What star is it?
It is the star of Israel
It has shone for a long time

The hat

He only wears it when it rains.
The hat
turns him into a rat.

His face peaks
beneath the narrow brown brim.
The hat swallows him up;

And turns him into
a bit-part crook;
into a Hollywood gangster;
into the man who works
for the Big Bad Boss.

If the rain doesn't stop soon
there'll be a shoot-out.

Well caught

These days I'm in love with my face.
It has grown round and genial as I've become older.
In it I see my grandfather's face and that
Of my mother. Yes – like a ball it has been thrown
From one generation to the next.

The man on the desert island

The man on the desert island
Has forgotten the ways of people,
His stories are all of himself.
Day in, day out of time
He communes with himself and sends
Messages in green bottles:
Help me they say *I am*
Cast up and far from home.
Each day he goes to watch
The horizon for ships.
Nothing reaches his shore
Except corked green bottles.

At night in the laundrette

I sit in the laundrette
Watch my reflection sitting
On the chequered pavement

The black wet street reflects
Moonmilk, primroses
A bus sails by, a boat
Festooned with lanterns

My shadow warms itself
By a red puddle
Hell's fire flickers there
Stirred by drops of rain

Shallow poem

I've thought of a poem.
I carry it carefully,
nervously, in my head,
like a saucer of milk;
in case I should spill some lines
before I can put it down.

John Agard

Introduction

A question that children like to ask is: 'Did you always want to be a poet?' The answer is 'No'. But as I try to remember what else I wanted to be, and as I look back at some of the things I enjoyed at school, I can now see a kind of pattern which has to do with the 'magic of words'.

This takes us back to Guyana, South America. I was a 'town boy', as the Guyanese people say, and grew up in the capital, Georgetown, with its Altantic coastline and lots of wooden houses. My primary school was called St Mary's RC and my secondary was St Stanislaus College.

Like so many boys who attended Roman Catholic schools, I had the idea of becoming a priest, maybe because my secondary school teachers were mostly priests, and at about 12 I used to serve mass as an 'altar boy'. At home I'd drape a long sheet around my shoulders and pretend to be a priest chanting Latin, while my cousin would be kneeling before me, pouring out a little wine pinched from an unsuspecting uncle.

Though I had no brothers or sisters, I grew up with lots of cousins and friends. Both boys and girls liked playing cricket, or Bat and Ball, as we called it. After being hit by a hard leather ball, I preferred sticking to a flannel ball.

You may be wondering what cricket has to do with becoming a poet. Well, in those days we had no television, and a famous cricket commentator was a man named John Arlott. When I was a little boy, I'd pretend to be a cricket commentator and try to sound like that same man on the radio. I'd speak of the 'gentle breeze' blowing across the field, the 'glorious sunshine', and balls being hooked 'majestically' to the boundary, bringing the West Indies score to something like 900 runs for the loss of only one wicket!

True, my imagination was running away with me, but looking back at those 'pretend commentaries' I can say now that something inside of me must have been excited by the power of words – the same power that was stirring something in me when I pretended to be the priest chanting Latin words. And cricket and the church certainly have one thing in common – a sense of drama, a sense of ritual.

At that age, I would never have imagined the priest as an

actor, but it shouldn't come as a surprise to hear that I wanted very much to become an actor, after I got my first part as Captain Hook in Peter Pan at about 14.

Whether priest, commentator or actor, words were casting their spell. At school, I enjoyed elocution, debating, and my favourite subject was English. Our English teacher was a priest, Father Maxwell – to us he was Maxy – and he made words come alive. Every day he'd write about six words from the dictionary on the blackboard. We had to copy these words in an exercise book, and sometimes he'd explain the meanings in a funny way. I'd make up little essays – or compositions – for him to read. I didn't always wait for him to give us homework, but when it came to subjects like Maths, Chemistry and Physics, I'd never remind our teacher about homework.

As far as I can remember, my earliest poems were written at about 16, and some were published in a sixth-form magazine called *Expression*. But even then, I do not have any clear memory of saying to myself, 'I'd like to be a poet'.

Back in those teenage years of going to lots of parties, the songs that I liked best were not just the ones with a catchy beat. No. The words were important. Soul music was popular at that time, and I can still hear Otis Redding, singing, 'I'd be the weeping willow drowning in my tears...'

Later, singers like Jimi Hendrix would excite me with lines like 'Excuse me, while I kiss the skies...'

Even then words were reaching out to me, though I wasn't thinking I'd be a poet. Or maybe there was a little jumbie (spirit) inside of me – you might call it an elf or a fairy – urging me on in the direction of words. Preparing the ground of my imagination so that poems would one day sprout.

FACT FILE

Birthplace	Guyana
School	St Mary's RC (primary), St Stanislaus College (secondary)
Favourite sport	Admire the artistry of test cricket, athletics, ice-skating and Sumo wrestling
Musical interest	When the mood gets me I play around and improvise on the flute
Favourite food	Curry, Guyanese cook-up rice, fish and chips
Favourite drink	Guinness
Best TV programme	Donahue late-night chat show
Travels abroad	Parts of the Caribbean, Russia, Canada, Germany, Singapore
Favourite books (as a child)	The *Hardy Boys* and *Nancy Drew* mysteries, *The Secret Seven* and *The Famous Five* series by Enid Blyton
Favourite poets	I get a special nourishment from oral poetry of cultures such as Eskimo, Chinese, Pygmy, North American Indian, and the lyrics of calypso
Comment on 'green' issues	I read once about writers in prison having to use toilet paper to write a novel, or a bar of soap on which to write a poem. After that I realised how much we take paper for granted in the same way we take water for granted. Without trees, without water, we're nothing
Preferred transport	Trains

Poetry jump-up

Tell me if ah seeing right
Take a look down de street

Words dancin
words dancin
till dey sweat
words like fishes
jumpin out a net
words wild and free
joinin de poetry revelry
words back to back
words belly to belly

Come on everybody
come and join de poetry band
dis is poetry carnival
dis is poetry bacchanal
when inspiration call
take yu pen in yu hand
if yu don't have a pen
take yu pencil in yu hand
if yu don't have a pencil
what the hell
so long de feeling start to swell
just shout de poem out

Words jumpin off de page
tell me if ah seeing right
words like birds
jumpin out a cage
take a look down de street
words shakin dey waist
words shakin dey bum
words wit black skin
words wit white skin
words wit brown skin
words wit no skin at all
words huggin up words

an sayin I want to be a poem today
rhyme or no rhyme
I is a poem today
I mean to have a good time

Words feeling hot hot hot
big words feeling hot hot hot
lil words feeling hot hot hot
even sad words cant help
tappin dey toe
to de riddum of de poetry band

Dis is poetry carnival
dis is poetry bacchanal
so come on everybody
join de celebration
all yu need is plenty perspiration
an a little inspiration
plenty perspiration
an a little inspiration

'Who the cap fit, let dem wear it'

If it wasn't you
who tek de chalk
and mark up de wall
juggle with de egg
and mek it fall
then why you didn't answer
when you hear Granny call?

It is wasn't you
who bounce yuh ball
in de goldfish bowl
wipe mud from yuh shoes
all over de floor
and poke yuh finger
straight in de butter

It it wasn't you
then why yuh heart a-flutter?
why yuh voice a-stutter?
and why you look so jumpy
when you stand up in front of Granny?

'Who the cap fit,
let dem wear it.'
That's what Granny does always say
and that she wasn't born yesterday.

The older the violin the sweeter the tune

Me Granny old
Me granny wise
stories shine like a moon
from inside her eyes.

Me Granny can dance
Me Granny can sing
but she can't play violin.

Yet she always saying,
'Dih older dih violin
de sweeter de tune.'

Me Granny must be wiser
than the man inside the moon.

Where does laughter begin?

Does it start in your head
and spread to your toe?

Does it start in your cheeks
and grow downwards so
till your knees feel weak?

Does it start with a tickle
in your tummy so
till you want to jump right out

of all your skin?
Or does laughter simply begin

with your mouth?

Prayer to laughter

O laughter
giver of relaxed mouths

you who rule our belly with tickles
you who come when not called
you who can embarrass us at times

send us stitches in our sides
shake us till the water reaches our eyes
buckle our knees till we cannot stand

we whose faces are grim and shattered
we whose hearts are no longer hearty
O laughter we beg you

crack us up
crack us up

The howdooyoodoo

Haven't you heard
of the how-doo-yoo-doo
how-doo-yoo-doo?

I'm surprised
you haven't heard
of the how-doo-yoo-doo
how-doo-yoo-doo

Spend a day or two
in a place called England
and I'm sure you'll meet
the how-doo-yoo-doo
how-doo-yoo-doo

But for those of you
without a clue
the how-doo-yoo-doo
is a creeping kind of plant
that takes you by the hand
and says how-doo-yoo-doo
how-doo-yoo-doo

And if by chance
you should say
I'm feeling down today
I got a tumour in my brain
and my old grandmother
keeps haemorrhaging
drops of rain
that doctors can't restrain

Then the how-doo-yoo-doo
gets embarrassed
almost a fright
retreats into itself
and begins to wither

So upon meeting
the how-doo-yoo-doo
this most peculiar plant
don't be alarmed
be polite
just take it by the hand
and say how-doo-yoo-doo
how-doo-yoo-doo
how-doo-yoo-doo
how-doo-yoo-doooooooooooooooooooo

One question from a bullet

I want to give up being a bullet
I've been a bullet too long

I want to be an innocent coin
in the hand of a child
and be squeezed through the slot
of a bubblegum machine

I want to give up being a bullet
I've been a bullet too long

I want to be a good luck seed
lying idle in somebody's pocket
or some ordinary little stone
on the way to becoming an earring
or just lying there unknown
among a crowd of other ordinary stones

I want to give up being a bullet
I've been a bullet too long

The question is
Can you give up being a killer?

Michael Rosen

Introduction

The whole of the time I was growing up, I thought I must be the most ordinary person in the world. I suppose I thought this because I read a huge number of books that were full of the extraordinary things that happened to people. They got involved with smugglers, or got whisked off to Australia or Africa. Me, all I seemed to do was sit about at home with my mum, my dad and my brother, or just go out and play with my friends. Nobody died, nobody was seriously ill, we didn't move, there were no earthquakes or disasters. It all seemed very, very ordinary.

The place where all this happened (!) was in a part of London called Pinner. We lived over a shop, but that wasn't because my mum and dad were shopkeepers; yet living there meant a lot of my life was to do with what went on behind and between shops. If you ever get to see behind a row of shops you'll see a higgledy-piggledy row of back yards, sheds, driveways and store-houses. That was my playground where I played with Keith Townsend, the butcher's son, and Johnny Calvert, the son of the manager of the International Stores. But the yards were full of grown-ups too; there was Baldy who was in charge of the builders yard, who always wore his blue boiler suit, there was the bank manager polishing his car, there was the antiques man who smoked cigars, his assistant who we called 'Accelerating-past-the-dustbins' because of the way he stopped his car by going faster before he jammed on the brakes. There was the cafe next door where they had a potato peeling machine in the yard. In the dirt and grit of the stony driveway we made beaches and castles and played five-stones on the drain covers, marked out goals and wickets, invented names for big stones, black stones, warty stones, lumpy stones and then ended up pelting each other with them.

My great friend was a boy called Brian Harrison, who I called Harrybo and we used to spend time together exploring a kind of open sewer called the River Pinn that ran past the shops and houses of Pinner. It was full of old springs, bike wheels, bottles, tin cans, packing cases, and filing cabinets and it ran through tunnels under the roads and along past the backs of people's houses, and you could look in and see them burning leaves in their gardens and eating crumpets, and watching TV. We were explorers, and singers, and cowboys and submarine commanders along there and we had risky meetings with park keepers, shop keepers, landlords and residents who were forever telling us we were either dangerous or in danger.

I went to a primary school that was mad keen on getting us to pass an exam called the eleven-plus which decided if you went to a grammar school, if you were good at exams, and a secondary modern if you weren't. Nearly every day was taken up with testing for maths, testing for English. We had places in the class and each week you moved your desk, so you always knew exactly who was better than you and who was worse. I remember joining in with other children and laughing at a girl because she was always 'bottom of the class'. I was always about the middle but really I wanted to be twelfth because the Twelfth Person sat nearest to the bell and got to ring it for playtime and end of school. I never made it.

I passed and went to Harrow Weald Grammar School. When I look back at my life, I think I was 'made' by the time I arrived there. I know I had to grow up and change but the person I was when I was about 11 or 12 feels rather like I am now. At this school I was very naughty, and was forever planning things to make teachers' lives difficult.

Somewhere about the age of 16 I decided I would like to write, and what got me started was reading the poems of D. H. Lawrence and the novels of James Joyce. Of course, I had done lots of writing as part of my school work and I had got the impression that teachers and my parents thought I could write well but now I thought I'd do some writing on my own. I started trying to read poetry and I found most of it intriguing but difficult and strange.

Well, I went to university, though on the way, I had this idea that I could become a doctor. At university I spent most of my time involved in acting, writing and directing plays but at the same time kept on trying to write poems about things that happened to me and things that had happened to me when I was a boy. My mother was doing radio broadcasts for schools at the time and she started putting some of my poems into her programmes. One day, the producer at the BBC, Joan Griffiths, said, 'Has Michael written any more?' I quickly wrote some more, sent them in and, next thing, she asked me if I would do a broadcast for her. Twenty years later, I'm still doing broadcasts with Joan.

These days, my life is like a jigsaw. No one day is like another. One day I might sit at home writing. The next I might be visiting a school and doing a performance, telling stories and poems to hundreds of children. The day after I might be doing some work with the radio or TV schools programmes. I might also be script-writing for the Children's Channel, on satellite TV. Then I might have to go and see publishers and look at the illustrations that have been done to go with what I've written. I love seeing what they've done and watching a book coming together. It's probably about as near as a man can get to having a baby. Some people think that's why men write, because they can't have babies!

Some people who read my books get bothered about whether what I write are poems. That's a shame. There are so many things in the world to get bothered about, and I always think that trying to make your mind up about whether something is a poem or a story doesn't matter at all. What matters is whether what you're reading tells you things that interest you or amaze you, or intrigue you or make you laugh. A word like 'poem' is only useful as a kind of label, like 'fruit' or 'vegetables'. What I'm trying to do is write things that explain to me how I came to do things in the way that I did and at the same time I hope they intrigue you and amuse you. It doesn't really matter what you call them, I'm certainly not bothered. But do you know, it bothered one teacher so much that she banned my books from her school. Strange world.

FACT FILE

Birthplace	Harrow, Middlesex
Brothers/sisters	One brother
Schools	Pinner Wood and West Lodge, Harrow Weald and Watford
Further education	Wadham College, Oxford University
Favourite sport	Athletics and football (support Arsenal)
Musical interest	Rhythm & Blues, soul, African music, folk music
Favourite food	Chick peas (curried), or chopped pickled herring
Favourite drink	Freshly-squeezed orange juice
Best TV programmes	French and Saunders, Ben Elton and Robbie Coltrane comedy
Best radio programme	Jazz FM
Travels abroad	France, Canada, Singapore, Australia
Favourite book (as a child)	*Tom Sawyer* by Mark Twain
Favourite poets	Carl Sandburg, Allan Ahlberg, Alice Walker, Siv Widerberg
Comment on 'green' issues	The world is destroyed by people who have the most power. Who has power? Politicians and people who own businesses. How can we get them to change? People who buy, who vote and people who work have to get together
Hobbies	Watching Arsenal
Collections	Books, pebbles, sea-worn bits of wood
Ambitions	Be asked to advise Arsenal how to win the League Championship again; speak French as well as a French person; be asked to live with my family in another country
Pets	Cat called 'Mickie'
Preferred transport	London buses and Inter-city trains

Harrybo

Once my friend Harrybo
came to school crying.

We said:
What's the matter?
What's the matter?
And he said
his grandad had died.

So we didn't know what to say.

Then I said:
How did he die?
And he said:
He was standing on St Pancras station
Waiting for the train
and he just fell over and died.

Then he started crying again.

He was a nice man
Harrybo's grandad.
He had a shed with tins full of screws in it.

Mind you,
my gran was nice too
she gave me and my brother
a red shoe horn each.

Maybe Harrybo's grandad gave
Harrybo a red shoe horn.

Dave said:
My hamster died as well.
So everyone said:
Shhhh.
And Dave said:
I was only saying.
And I said:
My gran gave me a red shoe horn.

Rodge said:
I got a pair of trainers for Christmas.
And Harrybo said:
You can get ones without laces.
And we all said:
Yeah, that's right, Harrybo, you can.

Any other day,
we'd've said:
Of course you can, *we* know that, you fool.
But that day
we said:
Yeah, that's right, Harrybo, yeah, you can.

My brother is making a protest about bread.
'Why do we always have wholemeal bread?
You can't spread butter on wholemeal bread
You try and spread the butter on
and it just makes a hole right through the middle.'

He marches out of the room and shouts
across the landing and down the passage.
'It's always the same in this place.
Nothing works.
The volume knob's broken on the radio you know
It's been broken for months and months you know.'

He stamps back into the kitchen
stares at the loaf of bread and says:
'Wholemeal bread – look at it, look at it.
You put the butter on
and it all rolls up.
You put the butter on
and it all rolls up.'

Over my toes

Over my toes
goes
the soft sea wash
see the sea wash
the soft sand slip
see the sea slip
the soft sand slide
see the sea slide
the soft sand slap
see the sea slap
the soft sand wash
over my toes.

The car trip

Mum says:
'Right, you two,
this is a very long car journey.
I want you two to be good.
I'm driving and I can't drive properly
if you two are going mad in the back.
Do you understand?'

So we say,
'OK Mum, OK. Don't worry,'
and off we go.

And we start The Moaning:
Can I have a drink?
I want some crisps.
Can I open my window?
He's got my book.
Get off me.
Ow, that's my ear!

And Mum tries to be exciting:
'Look out the window
there's a lamp-post.'

And we go on with The Moaning:
Can I have a sweet?
He's sitting on me.
Are we nearly there?
Don't scratch.
You never tell him off.
Now he's biting his nails.
I want a drink. I want a drink.

And Mum tries to be exciting again:
'Look out the window
there's a tree.'

And we go on:
My hands are sticky.
He's playing with the doorhandle now.
I feel sick.
Your nose is all runny.
Don't pull my hair.
He's punching me, Mum,
that's really dangerous, you know.
Mum, he's spitting.

And Mum says:
'Right I'm stopping the car.
I AM STOPPING THE CAR.'

She stops the car.

'Now, if you two don't stop it
I'm going to put you out the car
and leave you by the side of the road.'

He started it.
I didn't. He started it.

'I don't care who started it
I can't drive properly
if you two go mad in the back.
Do you understand?'

And we say:
OK, Mum, OK, don't worry.

Can I have a drink?

The Michael Rosen rap

You may think I'm happy, you may think I'm sad,
You may think I'm crazy, you may think I'm mad,
But hang on to your seats and listen right here
I'm gonna tell you something that'll burn your ear.

A hip. Hop. A hip hop hap.
I'm givin' you all the Michael Rosen rap.

I was born on the seventh of May
I remember very well that awful day
I was in my mother, curled up tight
Though I have to say, it was dark as night.
Nothing to do, didn't have to breathe,
I was so happy, didn't want to leave.

Suddenly, I hear some people give a shout:
One push, Mrs Rosen, and he'll be out.
I'm tellin' you all, that was a puzzle to me,
I shouted out, 'How do you know I'm a "he"?'
The doctor shouted, 'Good Lord, he can talk.'
I popped out my head, said, 'Now watch me walk.'
I juked and jived around that room,
Balam bam boola, balam de ditty boom.

A hip. Hop. A hip hop hap.
I'm givin' you all the Michael Rosen rap.

When I was one, I swam the English Channel,
When I was two, I ate a soapy flannel,
When I was three, I started getting thinner,
When I was four, I ate the dog's dinner,
When I was five, I was in a band playing drums,
When I was six, I ate a bag of rotten plums.
When I was seven, I robbed a bank with my sister,
When I was eight, I became Prime Minister,
When I was nine, I closed all the schools,
When I was ten, they made me King of the Fools.

So that's what I am, that's what I be
With an M, with an I, with a K, with an E.
That's what I am, that's what I be
Mr Mike, Mr Michael, Mr Rosen, Mr Me.
A hip. Hop. A hip hop hap.
I'm givin' you all the Michael Rosen rap.

It was spring in the fields and woods
the leaves in the hedges shook in the wind
as a crow stood quite still on a white horse's back.
He was looking at the grass about him
and the trees at the edge of the paddock
when all of a sudden he said to the horse beneath his feet:
Do you see how green everything is today?
and the horse said:
Well to tell you the truth – no, I don't.
everything looks pink to me
you see my eyes are pink ... he stopped.
the crow spoke again:
Oh. I'm sorry.
But how do you know that everything you see is pink
when it's the only colour you've ever seen?
The horse sat thinking about that for a while
and then said:
Well of course it's quite true what you say.
In fact I was only guessing.
But you see – when I was born,
everybody pointed at me and said: look at him –
his eyes are pink. So I thought everything I saw
was pink. It seemed a sensible thing to do at the time.
The crow shook his head slowly to and fro
breathed in deeply and sympathetically
and flew off to make his nest in the clear green sky.

Moira Andrew

Introduction

I'm what they call a late starter, a poet-come-lately. Although I've been writing since I can remember – poems, stories, letters, diaries – it was always for my eyes only. It simply did not occur to me that I might one day see my own name on the spine of a book. That was for *real* authors.

When I was a child I made up stories for my sister. Mostly they were serial stories with another exciting chapter every night at bedtime. Sometimes they ended abruptly when one or other of us fell asleep. One of these epics was called 'The Blue Highway'. I started to write it out in a school exercise book, then discovered what hard work this was and didn't finish it. I'd love to find the unfinished manuscript. One day I'll get around to writing that book for real.

My grandmother was the uncritical audience for my first poems. I remember sharing with her a poem called 'Sunrise'. It was summer. We sat in the sun at an upstairs window reading to the mesmeric sound of a roller going back and forth across the nearby tennis courts. I was eight.

At school, too, I was regarded as a 'good writer'. Sometimes I had to read my essays aloud to the rest of the class. They must have hated that, but Miss Anderson sat on her high chair nodding in approval. Once we had to make a poem into a story. It was about three children in a laundry basket pretending to be pirates. I wrote that one of the boys pointed to shore with 'a grubby forefinger'. This effort sent Miss Anderson into ecstasies.

There my writing career came to an end. I went to College, got married, had children, became a teacher. For years the idea of being a writer did not cross my mind.

I loved reading, of course, devouring books with all the appetite of a woolly mammoth. Work by contemporary poets was, and is, of enormous interest to me. I became head teacher of a primary school. I spent as much time as I could helping the children with their writing. One day a child brought me up with a jolt. 'What kind of poems do *you* write?' she asked. Good question. 'I haven't been doing much writing lately,' I said.

Then I saw an advertisement for a weekend course on poetry writing. I set off with high ambitions, well-sharpened pencils and a ream of A4 paper. Everyone else had brought along their collected works, fat folders jam-packed with poems. I was the only one without a piece of writing to share. I listened and learned.

I came home from that course sure that I too could be a published writer if I put my mind to it. Slowly I developed my own style, found my 'voice'. I sent work out to various small presses, most of which was promptly returned. Every writer knows the feeling.

'Rosie', a true piece about a baby, was the first poem I had published. I walked on air for days after I received that acceptance. Then began the serious business of writing for children, for adults, for teachers. I edited anthologies of poems for Juniors, taking on the near-impossible task of working on four books at once! My first collection of poems was published in 1986.

Now I am a freelance writer and no longer a teacher although I often visit schools to give readings and run writing workshops. When I'm not visiting schools I write. Routine is important and I try to be at my desk by 9.15 every morning. I never know what the next post or the next telephone call will bring. And there's always the next book to think about...

FACT FILE

Birthplace	Rutherglen, near Glasgow
Brothers/sisters	One sister who now lives in Australia
School	Glasgow High School for Girls
Further education	Jordanhill College of Education, Open University
Favourite sport	None ... except when Scotland play Wales at rugby
Musical interest	Listening to jazz
Favourite food	Home-baked bread, with lots of butter, fruit, curry, chocolate, cheese
Favourite drink	Coffee, black and strong, red wine
Best TV programmes	Documentaries, modern plays
Best radio programme	'Kaleidoscope'
Travels abroad	Switzerland, France, Spain, Malta
Favourite book (as a child)	*Anne of Green Gables* by L. M. Montgomery
Favourite poets	Brian Patten, Norman MacCaig, Gillian Clarke, Fleur Adcock, Maya Angelou, Douglas Dunn
Comment on 'green' issues	Hate litter. We could do much more to clean up towns, woodland, beaches
Hobbies	Collect fine old glass, pictures, children's reading books from 1930s
Ambitions	To write a best-selling novel, play the flute, travel around India
Pets	Siamese cat called 'Sammy'
Preferred transport	Car ... essential for a travelling poet

Act of worship

Every Sunday morning my grandmother
should have won a medal for bravery.
Every Sunday she dressed in her best,
walked to church on grandfather's arm.

They sat upstairs in the front pew
high above hats and nodding heads,
she in fur tippet, he in navy Sunday
suit, gold watch chain, topaz fob.

Every Sunday they stood up to sing.
No head for heights, Gran jammed the
backs of her knees against the seat,
her fine contralto faint with fear.

Sick, dizzy, she dared not look down.
'Why not tell him?' I asked. 'Oh, no,'
she said. 'Your grandfather says it's
the place to be. I'll get used to it.'

But she never did. She would produce
peppermints from a paper bag, hand
them round, part of the weekly ritual.
Grandfather bowed to acquaintances below.

Child with a cause

My grandmother was chicken-plump.
She wore long earrings, smelled of
Pear's soap and lavender water.
She kept cream in a jug under
a blue-beaded net.

Grandfather kept us both
on a tight rein, our place
at the kitchen sink. When Gran's mind
slipped slightly out of gear
I was her memory.

Nearly always, that is. She peeled
potatoes once, put them ready
for grandfather's tea and forgot
to light the gas. He was furious.
I saw Gran's tears.

Upstairs, in the narrow hall
I waited, scuffing the turkey-red rug.
He took his time. The flush thundered.
His shape vultured against
the door. I was raw

as carrion. 'It's not fair.
You made Gran cry.' He lunged at me.
'How dare you, child? How dare you
speak to me like that?' Picked clean
by anger I ran.

'Don't mind him,' my grandmother said.
'He likes his tea on time.' The matter
was closed. Grandfather tore into
his beef stew and mashed potatoes.
I pushed my plate away.

Shower

fierce
  spring
    rain
      full
        gushing
          drain
            grey
              puddled
drab   street
  steely   Wellies
  sky   for
    umbrellas   feet
    held
      high
        children
        want
cars   out
  make   harassed
   spray   mothers
    birds   shout
     huddle
    away
      cats
      lie
rain   asleep
  becomes   plants
   drops   drink
    slows   deep
   and
     stops
      doors
       open
        wide
         people
          step
           outside

Still Life

The day is deadlocked by heat.
Doors stand open all along
the street and telephones
are silent.
        A baby cries
in a thin half-hearted way
too hot to feed, too sweated
for sleep. Lawn mowers idle
in empty gardens; sprinklers
mizzle to themselves in great
pinwheels on the grass.
Washing hangs dead-crow limp
and flowers faint.
            I swing
slow circles of lettuce
in its wire basket, water
piddling warm over bare feet.

Lost, one Siamese cat

Like a stripped-down
engine, all his
working parts
are visible.

He wears his skin
like a speed-skater's suit,
gazes out from
blackcurrant eyes.

His face is all
triangles, black patent
nose, ears like
corner flags.

His whiskers sprout
from peppered holes;
yawning, his tongue is
a curling flame.

The most elegant
of cats, he steps with
Nureyev grace, purrs like
a thunderbox.

He pours himself
like cream from
window sill to puddle
of sunlight.

He has the voice
of a banshee, answers to
Sam. If found, return
to Jones, number 95,

PLEASE.

Letter from Egypt

Dear Miriam,
        Just a line
to let you know how things
are with us & of course to
thank you (& your good man)
for all you did for us – &
at your busiest time too
what with the census &
everything. I was quite
exhausted & the baby was
beginning to make himself
felt. If it hadn't been
for your help that night
my baby might have died.

  Good of you
to put up with all our
visitors – who'd have
thought, six scruffy
shepherds up & leaving
their sheep like that?
& didn't they ever smell?
Still they were good-
hearted & they meant well.
I hope they brought some
extra trade to the inn.
They looked in need of
a hot drink & a meal.

  & what about
those Kings, Miriam? Kneeling
there in their rich robes
& all? & me in nothing but
my old blue dress! Joseph
said not to worry, it was
Jesus they'd come to see.
Real gentlemen *they* were.
But what funny things to

give a baby – gold & myrrh
& frankincense. That's men
all over! It wouldn't cross
their minds to bring a shawl!

   Sorry we left
so suddenly. No time for
good-byes with King Herod on
the warpath! We had to take
the long way home & I'm so
tired of looking at sand!
Joseph has picked up a few
jobs mending this & that so
we're managing quite well.
Jesus grows bonnier every
day & thrives on this way
of life, but I can't wait
to see Nazareth again.

                    Love to all
                    at the inn,

          Mary

One parent family

My mum says she's clueless
not, as you'd imagine,
at wiring three pin plugs or
straightening a bicycle wheel,
but at sewing buttons
on a shirt, icing names and
dates on birthday cakes,
preparing a three-course meal.

She's not like other mothers;
although she's slim and neat
she looks silly in an apron,
just great in dungarees.
She'll tackle any household job,
lay lino, fix on tiles, does
all the outside paintwork, climbs
a ladder with practised ease.

Mind you, she's good for
a cuddle when I fall and
cut my knee. She tells me
fantastic stories every night,
laughs at *my* disasters, says
that she's as bad when she
reads a recipe all wrong and
her cakes don't come out right.

I know on Open Evenings
she gives a bad impression
at the school. She doesn't wear
the proper clothes. 'Too bad,'
the others sometimes say,
'you've got such a peculiar mum.'
'It's just as well,' I tell them.
'She is my mother *and* my dad!'

John Rice

Introduction

I was born in Glasgow in 1948 and grew up in Saltcoats, Ayrshire. I grew up sufficiently to be registered as a teenager. By that time The Beatles and The Rolling Stones were in the charts. Cliff Richard had a backing group then called The Shadows; they too had quite a few hits and I would spend hours with my collection of Shadows' records making up words and lyrics for them (nearly all their records were instrumentals which had strong melodies). At school I enjoyed three subjects in particular: English, French and Spanish. Spaceflight was just beginning to make the headlines in the early Sixties and the American astronauts and Russian cosmonauts were on television a lot. At school we talked about them in science classes – my hero was Yuri Gagarin, the first man in space.

These interests have remained with me and I am still very keen on space travel and astronomy, languages, words and writing. I've gone off The Shadows a bit though!

For many years I have been a keen runner. I train every day and I have competed in eight marathons, including the London Marathon. In 1989 I decided to rest – but I quickly became bored and took up the triathlon. In that sport you have to swim, cycle and run. It's just as hard as the marathon, but there's more variety. I like to keep fit: I do not smoke and I'm vegetarian. Mind you I do like the occasional Mars Bar (that's what they call the pubs on Mars).

Since I published my first book for children in 1982, *Zoomballoomballistic*, I have visited many schools to read and perform my 'Zoom Show' which is full of comic poems, stories and juggling.

Once I visited Warrington to do my 'Zoom Show' and I was very surprised when no one turned up to see it! Anyway, when I looked again at the advertising poster instead of 'The Zoom Show', it said 'The Doom Show' – no wonder no one came!

In my new book, *Bears don't like bananas*, the artist Charles Fuge has contributed wonderfully imaginative illustrations. It's another aspect of how poetry allies itself with other forms of communication ... recitation, performance and with art work.

FACT FILE

Birthplace	Glasgow, Scotland
Brothers/sisters	2 brothers
School	St Mary's Primary School in Saltcoats, and then St Michael's College in Ayrshire
Further education	Army School of Languages where I studied Arabic
Favourite sport	Athletics and cycling
Musical interest	Rock and pop, jazz, blues and classical music.
Favourite food	Vegetarian pasta sprinkled with lemon juice
Favourite drink	French mineral water
Best TV programme	M*A*S*H
Best radio programme	'Week ending'
Travels abroad	Widely in Europe, the Middle East
Favourite book (as a child)	*1001 questions answered about astronomy* by J. S. Pickering
Favourite poets	Dozens!
Comment on 'green' issues	My poem 'The Tourists' tries to show that we are causing harm to the animal world without even knowing about it
Hobbies	Collect books, and I have an interest in hundreds of subjects: archaeology, photography, astronomy, space flight...
Ambition	To travel to Jupiter
Preferred transport	Bicycle

Seaside song

It was a
sunboiled brightlight friedegg hotskin suntanned
sizzler of a day

It was a
popsong dingdong candyfloss dodgemcar spaceinvader
  beachwader
smashing seaside town

We had a
swelltime a welltime a realpellmelltime
a finetime a rhymetime a superdoubledimetime

We beachswam ate ham gobbledup a chicken leg
climbed trees chased bees
got stuck in mud up to our knees
played chase flew in space
beat a seagull in a skating race
rowed boats quenched throats
spent a load of £5 notes
sang songs hummed tunes
played hide-and-seek in sandy dunes
did all these things, too much by far,
that we fell asleep going back in the car...
from Folkestone.

The tourists

The sun sets like a glowing peach
on the holiday beaches.
All night the tourists have fun
dancing under the bright disco lights,
red, green, blue, glowing white, sparkling silver.
They dance to the rhythms of today's top ten.

But just offshore, in the shallow bay,
the giant loggerhead turtle swims unseen,
terrorised by this wild music,
frightened by the flashing lights,
too scared to wade ashore to lay her eggs.

For two nights she has tried
to crawl from sea to sand to dig an egg-nest
with her ungainly paddle paws.
But the tourists and the teenagers
light beach fires for their barbecues
and their motorbikes scream with menacing voices.
The turtle is frightened.

Her mate is dying: some nights ago
he bravely came ashore but made the mistake
of eating a discarded plastic bag
not knowing it could damage an animal's stomach.
Now he cannot feed and he is in constant pain.

Just under the surface of the blue bay
the giant loggerhead turtles tread water.
No more than a quarter of a mile away
they remain unseen.
Blind as rocks and deaf as sand the tourists
continue with their cheap fun.
On and on, into the night, into the morning,
into the fate of the future.

Silver grey

a silver grey ripple
on
a grey silver river:
the squirrel crosses the road

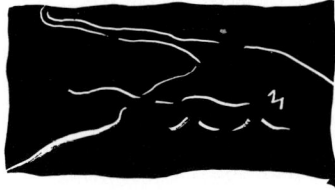

Mr McGhie's dictionary

Now and again I go next door
and ask to borrow Mr McGhie's dictionary.
He says he's always pleased
to lend it to me because
he rarely uses it.
Perhaps that's because he knows all the words.

He half closes the door and takes it down
from a high shelf beside the electric meter
(Mr McGhie is very tall and very thin –
he eats Polo mints all the time)
he blows the dust off the cover
and hands the book to me.
It's as heavy as a packed sports bag.
'There,' he says, 'see what marvels and mysteries
you can find in that.'

And I do.

It's an old dictionary – it doesn't
have words like 'space shuttle' or 'moonshot',
'hamburger', 'data bank', or 'breakdance'.
But you'll find millions of words to learn
and zillions of words that sound just right
for their meaning – like these for instance –
a 'flibbertigibbet' is a gossiping, restless person:
a 'papoose' which means a Red Indian child.
I love discovering words like these
in Mr McGhie's dictionary.

Sometimes I make up my own words out of the book:
try this!
THINGUMMYJIGGERYWHATCHMACALLITWHOJAMAFLIPPERY
THINGUMMYBOB

Mr McGhie knows I love this dictionary
– he sees me sitting on the doorstep in the sun
reading through the section about foreign languages.
'You still not got to the letter Z yet?'
he says with a kind of smile on his face.
He once said that if he died I could
have his dictionary so now I fetch his
Polo mints from the shop for him.

And if I have a child, or some children,
I'll read the words out to them.
Words that just sound good: words like
smithereens, plasmodium, memory, expunge,
goblin, orang-utan, barracuda, apfelstrudel,
zing, flip-flop, vulcanic, quango, Ramadan.

Words that were once secrets
in Mr McGhie's dictionary.

December day

White snow on a wide field,
ice blue the endless sky:

the sun in a Wedgwood eggcup.

A gift from the stars

On Christmas Eve, on the first chime of midnight,
the Christmas King and the Queen of Christmas
take the new moon, sharp as a blade,
and slit the thin paper sky.

They help each other wrap up the frosty stars
in the night's dark blue wrapping paper;
the Queen stretches out her sparkling hand
and grasps a passing comet to use as a gift tag.

The Queen of Christmas and the Christmas King
then take their present on a long journey:
   they slide past the icy meteorites
   they glide between the glassy suns,
   they slink in and out of cosmic clouds,
   they skim the outer edges of planets' rings
making their way through the caves and caverns of space
to this shining Earth
to this cold country
to this snowy town
to this still street
to this sleeping house
to this quiet bedroom
to this soft bed
and place their sky gift on your pillow.

And ping!
the second you open your eyes on Christmas morn
the parcel bursts open without a sound
and showers you with frosty stars
that zing and spin and melt and split and vanish
to become minuscule molecules of happiness.

And because children wake up so early
on Christmas Day (usually while it's still dark)
they never see this remarkable scientific phenomenon.

Poets' choice of poems from the past

Buffalo Bill's

Buffalo Bill's
defunct
          who used to
            ride a watersmooth-silver
                                    stallion
and break onetwothreefourfivepigeonsjustlikethat
                                                        Jesus

he was a handsome man
                        and what i want to know is
how do you like your blueeyed boy
Mister Death

e. e. cummings (1894–1962)

Gareth Owen comments...

Why
        he could write a poem
so smooth and simple easy
it made you think it came
on the same breath
he'd use for buying six packs
at the High Street A & P.
i tell you
            he wrote this poem one time
tells how this cowboy
comes to die
                well
he tells the tale so simple
                        so natural
just thinking of it
makes me weep
and now
        he's dead himself
that one day wrote that poem
and doesn't that just stop
and make you think?
and what i want to say is this
he wrote so smooth
so just like talk
it fools you into thinking
why
anyone could write that way

but isn't that
the trick of it
and haven't i
just proved
it isn't so.

The flower-fed buffaloes

The flower-fed buffaloes of the spring
In the days of long ago,
Ranged where the locomotives sing
And the prairie flowers lie low:-
The tossing, blooming, perfumed grass
Is swept away by the wheat,
Wheels and wheels and wheels spin by
In the spring that still is sweet.
But the flower-fed buffaloes of the spring
Left us, long ago.
They gore no more, they bellow no more,
They trundle around the hills no more:-
With the Blackfeet, lying low,
With the Pawnees, lying low,
Lying low.

Vachel Lindsay (1879–1931)

Judith Nicholls comments . . .

I love poetry that really *sings* and Vachel Lindsay is especially good at making words sing. Here the song is a sad one and what he wants to tell us is reflected beautifully in the slow fall of the final lines. Like all the best poems, it needs to be said *aloud*.

Ozymandias

I met a traveller from an antique land
Who said: Two vast and trunkless legs of stone
Stand in the desert... Near them, on the sand,
Half sunk, a shattered visage lies, whose frown,
And wrinkled lip, and sneer of cold command,
Tell that its sculptor well those passions read
Which yet survive, stamped on these lifeless things,
The hand that mocked them, and the heart that fed:
And on the pedestal these words appear:
'My name is Ozymandias, king of kings:
Look on my works, ye Mighty, and despair!'
Nothing beside remains. Round the decay
Of that colossal wreck, boundless and bare
The lone and level sands stretch far away.

Percy Bysshe Shelley (1792–1822)

Charles Causley comments . . .

A witty and beautifully observed comment
on boastfulness and self-aggrandizement.

Composed upon Westminster Bridge

Earth has not anything to show more fair:
Dull would he be of soul who could pass by
A sight so touching in its majesty:
This City now doth like a garment wear
The beauty of the morning; silent, bare,
Ships, towers, domes, theatres, and temples lie
Open unto the fields, and to the sky;
All bright and glittering in the smokeless air.
Never did sun more beautifully steep
In his first splendour, valley, rock, or hill;
Ne'er saw I, never felt, a calm so deep!
The river glideth at his own sweet will:
Dear God! the very houses seem asleep;
And all that mighty heart is lying still!

William Wordsworth (1770–1850)

Gerda Mayer comments ...

'So touching in its majesty.' This could describe the poem itself.
There is a stateliness combined with great lyricism here; a
serenity and luminosity. It has often, in the past, made me think
of Vermeer's painting 'View of Delft'.

FROM Song of myself

A child said *What is the grass?* fetching it to me
  with full hands.
How could I answer the child? I do not know what
  it is any more than he.
I guess it must be the flag of my disposition,
  out of hopeful green stuff woven.

Or I guess it is the handkerchief of the Lord,
A scented gift and remembrancer designedly dropt,
Bearing the owner's name someway in the corners,
  that we may see and remark, and say *Whose?*

Or I guess the grass is itself a child, the produced
  babe of the vegetation.

Walt Whitman (1819–1892)

John Agard comments . . .

These lines were written over 100 years ago but they still have something fresh and clean like wet grass. I especially like the image or picture of grass as God's handkerchief because it makes grass, which we take for granted, become magical. These lines make me feel part of the bigger mystery that is life.

This is a speech that comes from a play called 'The Tempest' by William Shakespeare, written four hundred years ago. The person speaking is called Caliban and he is the person who has always lived on the island. But a powerful and clever man called Prospero and his daughter Miranda come to settle there too. Here, Caliban is talking to Prospero.

From The Tempest

Caliban: This island's mine, by Sycorax my mother,
      Which thou tak'st from me. When thou cam'st first,
      Thou strok'st me, and made much of me; wouldst give me
      Water with berries in't; and teach me how
      To name the bigger light, and how the less,
      That burn by day and night: and then I lov'd thee,
      And show'd thee all the qualities o'th' isle,
      The fresh springs, brine-pits, barren place and fertile:
      Curs'd be I that did so! All the charms
      Of Sycorax, toads, beetles, bats, light on you!
      For I am all the subjects that you have,
      Which first was mine own King: and here you sty me
      In this hard rock, whiles you do keep from me
      The rest o' th' island.

William Shakespeare (1564–1616)

Michael Rosen comments . . .

In 1987 I went to Australia and heard speeches from the
aboriginal peoples of Australia who were saying the same sort of
things as Caliban is saying here and, in turn, have been said by
native Americans, Africans, Indians and many other people all
over the world.

   Later, Caliban tells of what it feels like to live in such a place
and he thinks wonderful things are possible but he wakes up to
find nothing.

Caliban: Be not afeard; the isle is full of noises,
      Sounds and sweet airs, that give delight, and hurt not.
      Sometimes a thousand twangling instruments
      Will hum about mine ears; and sometime voices,
      That, if I then had wak'd after long sleep,
      Will make me sleep again: and then, in dreaming,
      The clouds methought would open, and show riches
      Ready to drop upon me; that, when I wak'd,
      I cried to dream again.

OM THE PAST • POETS' CHOICE OF POEMS FROM THE PAST • POETS' CHOICE OF POEM

The witch

I saw her plucking cowslips,
  And marked her where she stood:
She never knew I watched her
  While hiding in the wood.

Her skirt was brightest crimson,
  And black her steeple hat.
Her broomstick lay beside her –
  I'm positive of that.

Her chin was sharp and pointed,
  Her eyes were – I don't know –
For, when she turned towards me –
  I thought it best – to go!
                    Percy H. Hott

Moira Andrew comments . . .

I used to recite this poem as a child. It's perhaps not the best
poem in the world, but I loved the sense of mystery and colour
. . . 'skirt was brightest crimson', and 'black her steeple hat'. And,
of course, the cowslips. I'd never actually seen a cowslip but I
liked the sound of the word and the picture it made in my head.

Ca' the Yowes

Ca' the yowes to the knowes,
Ca' them where the heather grows,
Ca' them where the burnie rows,
  My bonnie dearie.

Hark! the mavis' evening sang
Sounding Clouden's woods amang;
Then a-faulding let us gang,
  My bonnie dearie.

We'll gae down by Clouden side,
Thro' the hazels spreading wide
O'er the waves that sweetly glide
  To the moon sae clearly.

Yonder's Clouden's silent towers,
Where at moonshine midnight hours,
O'er the dewy-bending flowers,
  Fairies dance sae cheery.

Ghaist nor bogle shalt thou fear;
Thou'rt to love and Heaven sae dear,
Nocht of ill may come thee near,
  My bonnie dearie.

Fair and lovely as thou art,
Thou hast stown my very heart;
I can die – but canna part,
  My bonnie dearie.

Robert Burns (1759–1796)

John Rice comments...

When I attended school in Ayrshire we learned many of Robert Burns' poems and although we didn't understand the old words and the forgotten dialect we understood what he was saying through the simplicity and beauty of his words. Burns was always 'a poet of the people' and in Scotland his poems and songs are still recited and sung at parties, weddings and family gatherings.

   'Ca' the yowes' is a love poem that draws on the imagery of farming and nature – subjects that Burns knew well. The poem has been set to music and I often feel a sense of sadness when I hear it – perhaps because we don't know if the person Burns wrote it for loved him in return.

Write your own poems

Having read the poems in this book, now have a go at writing
your own. A useful way 'in' is to begin by building-up the
structure of your poem. You can start with familiar objects.

Creating poems

Begin by thinking about a house. What do we call a large house?
A palace . . . manor . . . mansion. Let's select mansion. Imagine
the mansion has been unoccupied for years. The furniture
remains in place, but no one has lived there for a long time. You
are given the key. You decide to explore the deserted mansion.

The title comes easily – 'The Deserted Mansion'. Now enter the
hall. Make *four* observations about what you see and what you
hear. Write down one observation per line. This creates verse 1.

> Grey cobwebs hang from the ceiling,
>   Old antlered hatstand is made of teak,
> Maroon carpet half-eaten by moths,
>   Dusty floorboards creak, creak, creak.

Note the use of rhyme at the end of lines 2 and 4 – 'teak' . . .
'creak'.

Now add a chorus, concentrating on the temperature in the
hall.

> Cold, draughty house.
> Chilly, freezing place.

Verse 1 is now complete. It can be written like this:

The Deserted Mansion

1 The hall

> Grey cobwebs hang from the ceiling,
>   Old antlered hatstand is made of teak,
> Maroon carpet half-eaten by moths,
>   Dusty floorboards creak, creak, creak.
>   Cold, draughty house.
>   Chilly, freezing place.

120

Choose another room in the house (the kitchen? the cellar?) and make your *four* observations. You can now proceed with verse 2. And thereafter, verses 3, 4, 5 . . .

A–Z poems

An A–Z is another structure, and is a bit of a brain-teaser. The idea is to complete your poem in just 26 words. The first word begins with the letter A, the second word with the letter B, and so on until you reach Z.

'An A–Z of Newspaper Headlines' uses a number plan with four words per line.

> Atomic Blast Cripples Doncaster
> Embittered Farmer Garrottes Hooligans
> Injured Judge's Kidney – Lost
> Mad Nun Ousts Pope
> Queen Rewrites Shakespeare's Tragedies
> Ugly Vicar Worships Xylophone
> Yellow Zebra!

Write your own 'A–Z of Sport Headlines' (or disaster headlines, or horror headlines) using the same verse structure.

As an alternative, try an 'A–Z of New Names for Pop Groups'. The structure is different. Give your poem a particular shape on the page.

> Armed Bandits
> Creepy Dracula
> Egg Flops
> Ghost Hunters
> (and so on)

Poems about simple objects

A box – a simple box – offers further scope for poems. What
creatures lurk inside the small, closed box? Ant? Dragonfly?
Woodlouse? Gnat? Centipede? Spider? Quite quickly you will be
able to think of a couple of dozen. Now give each creature a
colour, and also a single word to indicate what it is doing inside
the box. Verse 1 can be written out like this:

> Open the box
> and you will find
> a scarlet ant wandering,
> a purple millipede snoozing,
> a pink butterfly fluttering,
> a white worm wriggling,
>   inside the box,
>   inside the box.

There are eight lines in the verse. Four lines are short, and four
lines are long. Keeping the pattern the same, write verse 2. The
short lines remain the same. Make sure you don't use a colour
twice. Also, note the fourth long line: 'a white worm wriggling'.
Beginning each word with the same letter – in this case 'w' – is
very effective. This technique is called 'alliteration'. Do the same
in verse 2. Choose 'spider' as the creature in the box.

Haikus

The haiku is a well-known poem form. It is very short, having
just three lines. Each line comprises a strict syllable count.

Line 1	5 syllables
Line 2	7 syllables
Line 3	5 syllables
Total	17 syllables

Here is an example:

Fox

Slinks to the wood's edge
and – with one paw raised – surveys
the open meadows.

Count the syllables.
Now write your own haiku poem. Take the title 'A small, dark place'. It could be the inside of a pocket, or the bottom of a swing bin, or behind the fridge. The idea is for you to create a complete 'mini' world in 17 syllables.

Because the haiku is short you can easily rewrite the poem a number of times (drafting), thus improving the quality of your word usage.

Word pictures

Word pictures (or images) play a big part in poetry. John Rice's poem 'A gift from the stars' (page 102) creates wonderful visual effects for the reader. Make you own word pictures by writing about the moon. Think about what the moon looks *like*. The moon, of course, has different shapes: round, half circle, crescent. Don't forget to include the night sky (darkness, clouds, stars) in your extended image writing. As we have seen before, it helps if you follow a verse structure.

The Moon is like ...

The Moon is like
   a saucer of milk
waiting to be lapped
   by a black cat.

The Moon is like
   a fingernail clipping
lying on the dark tiles
   of the bathroom floor.

Automatic writing

Feelings and emotions are another important ingredient in
poems. An example is Judith Nicholls' poem 'The dare' (page 32).
For once, ignore poem structure and write freely. Think about
something that has saddened you, or angered you, or disturbed
you. You might choose to write about an international disaster
(famine, flood, volcanic eruption, terrorism), or a private sadness
(death of pet). Allow your pen or pencil to write non-stop on the
paper. This is called 'automatic writing'. The intention is to allow
your feelings to flow freely and to fully express yourself.

Once the writing is finished, rewrite the piece, selecting and
reorganising the material. This is your second draft. It should
turn out more polished than the first effort. The third draft
should see the poem really take shape. All of this is hard work
and requires effort and concentration. The end result – a
completed, polished, refined poem on the page – gives you a good
feeling of achievement.

Index of first lines

Acknowledgements

The series editor and publisher would like to thank the following for permission to reproduce poems:

Gareth Owen 'Salford Road' from *Salford Road and other poems* and 'My sister Betty', 'Song of the city', 'Out in the city' and 'A dog's life' from *Song of the City*, both anthologies published by Young Lions, Collins; 'In Henley Library' © Gareth Owen. All poems reproduced by permission of Rogers, Coleridge & White Ltd.

Judith Nicholls 'Countdown' © Judith Nicholls 1989. First published in *What On Earth* compiled by Judith Nicholls, published by Faber and Faber, and reprinted by permission of the author. 'Hermitage Woods' and 'Give me your name' © Judith Nicholls 1990. First published in *Dragonsfire* by Judith Nicholls, published by Faber and Faber, and reprinted by permission of the author. 'Moonscape' from *Magic Mirror* by Judith Nicholls, reprinted by permission of Faber and Faber Ltd. 'A poem from the rainforest' and 'The dove' from *Midnight Forest* by Judith Nicholls, reprinted by permission of Faber and Faber Ltd.

Charles Causley 'Forbidden games', 'My enemy', 'Logs of wood', 'At St Hilary', 'Tom Bone' from *Collected Poems* by Charles Causley, published by Macmillan and reproduced by permission of David Higham Associates and the author.

Gerda Mayer 'Fragment', 'Hide and seek', 'Well caught', 'Star of sorrow', 'The hat', 'The man on the desert island', 'At night in the laundrette', 'Shallow poem' reproduced by permission of the author.

John Agard 'Poetry jump-up', 'Who the cap fit, led dem wear it', 'The older the violin the sweeter the tune', 'Where does laughter begin?', 'Prayer to laughter', 'The howdooyoodoo' and 'One question from a bullet' reproduced by permission of the Caroline Sheldon Literary Agency and the author.

Michael Rosen 'Over my toes' from *Smelly Jelly, Smelly Toes* by Michael Rosen and Quentin Blake. Text © 1986 Michael Rosen. Illustrations © 1986 Quentin Blake. Published in the UK by Walker Books Limited. 'My brother is making . . .', and 'It was spring in the fields . . .' from *Mind Your Own Business* by Michael Rosen, published by Andre Deutsch Ltd. 'Harrybo', 'The car trip' and 'The Michael Rosen rap' from *The Hypnotiser*, published by Andre Deutsch Ltd, reproduced by permission of Scholastic Publications Ltd.

Moira Andrew 'One parent family', 'Act of worship', 'Child with a cause', 'Shower', 'Still life', 'Lost, one Siamese cat' and 'Letter from Egypt' reproduced by permission of the author.

John Rice 'Seaside song', 'The tourists', 'Silver grey', 'Mr McGhie's dictionary', 'December day' and 'A gift from the stars' reproduced by permission of the author.

'Buffalo Bill's' from *Collected Poems* by e.e. cummings, published by McGibbon & Kee, an imprint of Harper Collins Publishers Limited, reproduced by permission of Harper Collins Publishers Ltd.